COLOR
UNDER GROUND

A Scribner Portfolio in Natural History

COLOR
UNDER GROUND

The Mineral Picture Book

Photographs by
Lee Boltin

Text by
John S. White, Jr.

Charles Scribner's Sons • **New York**

Photograph on page 1:
   Sulfur • orthorhombic • sulfur
   Agrigento, Sicily, Italy
Photograph on page 2:
   Pyrite • isometric • iron sulfide
   Fort Scott, Bourbon County, Kansas

Printed in the United States of America
SBN 684-12384-3
Library of Congress Catalog Card Number 75-143948

Acknowledgments
   The many suggestions of Dr. Joel E. Arem of
the Smithsonian Institution were extremely
helpful in preparing the text and are gratefully
acknowledged. All the minerals shown in this
book are in the collections of the National
Museum of Natural History, Smithsonian Institution, Washington, D.C.

COLOR
UNDER GROUND

Since man first appeared on the earth he has made use of earth materials—the minerals and rocks he found in caves, stream beds, and mountain cliffs. The first geologist was probably a cave man who wondered at the glitter of a pretty pebble and perhaps broke it open to see what might be inside.

The crust of the earth is made up of rocks, and the rocks themselves are made of minerals. Just as cakes or other culinary products consist of specific ingredients in fixed amounts, the various types of rocks are made up of minerals of fixed composition, in more or less specific amounts. The makeup of rocks is less rigidly defined than is the composition of minerals.

Some kinds of rocks consist of only one mineral; for example, marble and limestone are composed of the single mineral calcite. Quartzite is a rock made up of cemented grains of the mineral quartz, and often the cement itself is also quartz. Some types of minerals contain metals, which are easily released and concentrated by heating or chemical processes, and large occurrences of such economically important minerals are called ore deposits.

A mineral may be defined as a naturally occurring solid with a fixed chemical composition, but this definition is flexible enough to allow for slight variations in chemistry in a given mineral species. In spite of their diversity, all minerals share a common characteristic: their constituent atoms are arranged in a regular and periodic way. This type of pervasive orderliness is an essential feature of all solid materials and is a result of the directional nature of the forces that bind atoms together.

The earth is a vast chemical laboratory in which all the elements interact in a great variety of environments, both chemical and physical. Over 2,000 different minerals are known today, and more are being discovered every year. Some widely known minerals are quartz, diamond, graphite, talc, and gypsum. Each has a distinctive composition and arrangement of the atoms of which it is composed. The composition of quartz is silicon dioxide, shown in chemical symbols as SiO_2. This means that for every silicon atom (Si) in quartz there are two oxygen atoms, and the positioning of these atoms is characteristic of the mineral. Two minerals may have the same composition but a different arrangement of atoms; in that case, the two are considered different minerals. Diamond and graphite, both composed only of carbon, are good examples. Their structural dissimilarity is revealed in the fact that diamond is the hardest mineral and graphite one of the softest.

One common characteristic of minerals is that they often occur in crystals. A crystal is a solid bounded by naturally formed plane faces, representing the limits of growth of the crystal. Few classes of natural objects have aroused as much interest, delight, and wonder as the group of solids that occur in sparkling, multifaceted crystals. The perfection of crystal forms, the mirrorlike surfaces of crystal faces, the intensity and depth of color have all conspired to place crystals among the most awe-inspiring of nature's curiosities. They are no less intriguing to the scientist who understands many of their secrets than to the novice viewing mineral crystals for the first time. To the trained observer, crystals are a storehouse of information about their composition and the history of their growth, yet they can provide visual pleasure to anyone with an eye for the beauty of natural forms.

Like other objects which scientists study, crystals have been classified and grouped according to a scheme. They are usually classified according to the symmetry they possess. Symmetry can best be understood by regarding it as a regular repetition of some feature, such as a crystal face. For example, a cube has six faces, all square and of identical size. If a cube is rotated about a line drawn through the centers of opposite cube faces, the other four square faces can be seen to parade into and out of view when observed at right angles to the axis of rotation. If the rotation were stopped every 90 degrees, one could not tell merely on the basis of the cube's appearance that it had been rotated at all. This visual identity of different aspects of a crystal is the means for identifying symmetrically related crystal faces.

The number of symmetries that can exist in solids is rather limited. When all known minerals are classified according to their symmetry, only seven types can be distinguished. These seven symmetry groups, or "crystal systems," are known as the isometric (sometimes called cubic), tetragonal, orthorhombic, monoclinic, triclinic, hexagonal, and rhombohedral systems; they are discussed in more detail on pages 14-24. The rhombohedral system is sometimes considered a subclass of the hexagonal. The various terms used to describe the different types of crystal faces constitute the basis of crystal morphology. The study of morphology (from the Greek word for "form") is concerned with the outward appearance of crystals. Since crystals

Basic forms of the seven crystal systems

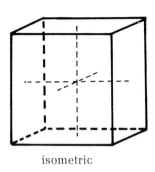

isometric

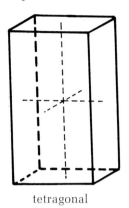

tetragonal

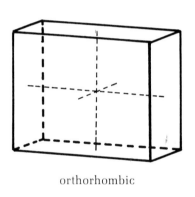

orthorhombic

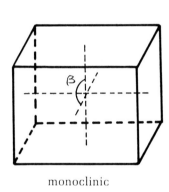

monoclinic

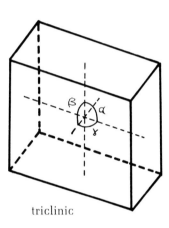

triclinic

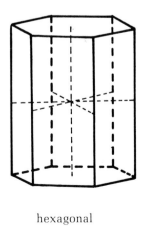

hexagonal

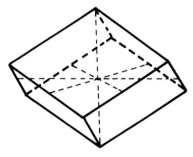

rhombohedral

Examples of isometric forms

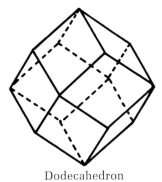

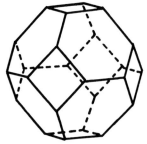

Dodecahedron

Cube and octahedron

Examples of tetragonal forms

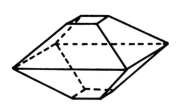

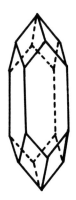

Pyramid and base

Pyramid and prism

Examples of orthorhombic forms

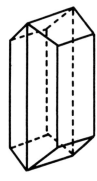

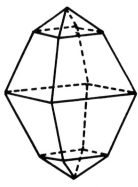

Prisms and base

Two pyramids

10

Examples of monoclinic forms

Prisms and base

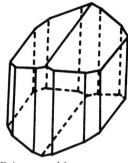

Prisms and bases

Examples of triclinic forms

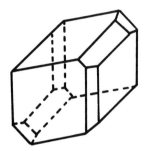

Prisms and bases

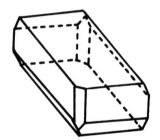

Prisms and bases

Example of hexagonal forms

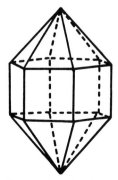

Pyramid and prism

Example of rhombohedral forms

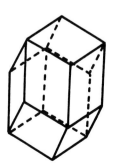

Rhombohedron and prism

11

are bounded by plane faces, the terminology largely involves the description and naming of various types of faces.

Crystal symmetry is usually described in terms of forms. A form is a set of crystal faces all related in the same way to imaginary reference lines within the crystal. These lines, called the crystal axes, have specific lengths for each mineral and make specified angles with one another.

The diagrams on page 9 illustrate the basic forms characteristic of the crystal systems. Faces are usually described in terms of indices, which are sets of numbers derived from the orientations of the faces with respect to the imaginary crystal axes. In three dimensions, the axes consist of three intersecting reference lines (four in the case of the hexagonal system), not all lying in the same plane, which suffice to create space-filling blocks. In the isometric system (represented by the cube), the reference lines are all at right angles and are all the same length. The other crystal systems are characterized by different combinations of axial lengths and angles of intersection (see pages 10 and 11).

Minerals can form in a variety of ways. In some types of rocks, the ones arising deep within the earth, all the constituent minerals were once melted together. As the rock cooled, first one type of crystal, then another, formed, all in sequence, until the rock was completely solidified or crystallized. The various minerals making up the rock can often be observed with the naked eye.

Some minerals are formed when great pressures act within the earth, the same pressures that force flat-lying rock strata into crumpled mountain masses. These pressures may be great enough to melt rocks in small patches or else to force the chemical elements in the rocks to move about and seek new combinations among themselves.

Many of the more familiar minerals are deposited from solutions. If sea water is evaporated in a jar, a dry crust made up of a mixture of salts remains. Solutions in the earth contain many other types of salts, and such liquids deep underground may exist at high temperatures. If these so-called hydrothermal (literally, hot water) solutions travel toward the surface and begin to cool, minerals separate out. The process of growth is so slow that rather perfect, and sometimes very large, crystals have a chance to form. The environment of deposition of a mineral, then, is usually an opening or fissure underground, through which pass solutions that are discarding dissolved material in the form of crystals. The growth of these crystals is influenced by the many possible changes in the solution itself—changes in temperature, pressure, flow of the liquid—and by the nature of the rocks through which the solution is moving—composition, size of the openings, and so forth.

Mineral crystals have been found displaying almost all possible combinations of forms and representing all of the crystal systems. Sometimes crystals occur as single individuals with simple, bright, lustrous faces. In other cases they present curved and irregular or uneven faces quite unlike the ideal forms. In a non-ideal crystal, the form may be the cube, for example, but the "shape" would not be a perfect cube because of the tendency toward deformation. Deformed crystals are misleading, in that they do not exhibit their true symmetry—the symmetry of the mineral's atomic structure. Such external distortions are due largely to the influence of the complex environments in which minerals form. The vagaries of nature may act to produce crystal freaks and anomalies, to the delight of mineral collectors and the dismay of students of crystallography.

An endless range of colors and patterns exists in the mineral world. Intergrowth of two or more minerals, inclusions of one in another, coloration by impurities, and rhythmic, periodic deposition, all contribute to a kaleidoscopic variety of combinations.

Some minerals form twins, which are intergrowths of two or more crystals according to specific geometric laws. Many types of twins are known, and the twin laws which govern the angles at which crystals join are based on the symmetry characteristics of the various systems. Twinning on a microscopic scale is very common among minerals and poses one of the more baffling problems of mineralogical research.

Minerals most commonly occur as aggregates of crystals, with myriad individuals combining in parallel, intersecting, or radial patterns. Sometimes the individual crystals are so tiny as to be almost indistinguishable, but occasionally crystal groups are found in which individuals measure several feet in length.

Sometimes one mineral is replaced by another, with the outward form of the first mineral preserved. The resulting object is called a pseudomorph (false form), because the crystal shape observed is not that of the replacing mineral. Certain types of aggregates resemble replacements of organic remains and are thus confused with fossils (which actually are the petrified remains of living things). Such pseudo-replacements are often quite beautiful and constitute unusual objects for study.

In the following sections various types of mineral forms are discussed and illustrated. The specimens pictured have been chosen as much for their esthetic qualities as for the characteristics they admirably exemplify. Viewing them, one can readily understand the fascination that minerals have for both scientists and amateur collectors.

The numbers in parentheses in the text refer to the photographs which are numbered consecutively through the book and grouped following the text in the various sections. In the photograph captions, the first lines contain the name of the mineral, its crystal system, its chemical composition, and the location at which the specimen was found. For some specimens (39, 40, 42, 44) no crystal system is given, because there are no obvious crystals.

Simple Crystals

Most environments of crystal growth lack sufficient space for the development of complete individuals bounded on all sides by lustrous plane faces. Because of their relative rarity, single crystals are highly prized. If such crystals are not badly deformed, the symmetry they exhibit will reflect the arrangement of the atoms of which the crystals are made.

As mentioned earlier, every crystal can be assigned to one of seven systems and described in terms of "building block" units of specific shapes. Each system has a characteristically shaped block; the edges that intersect at a corner of each block may be thought of as imaginary lines, called axes, that define the shape of the block. To do this, the axes must have specific lengths and make definite angles with one another. The names of the crystal systems are derived from Greek words and refer to the lengths and/or inclinations of the axes.

In the isometric system (from the Greek *isometres,* of equal measure), the axes are all the same length and they meet at right angles. The cube is a form in which the faces are perpendicular to the crystal axes, and so the adjacent faces of a cube all lie at right angles to each other.

A great number of minerals form in the isometric system. These exhibit highly symmetrical crystals. The most common sulfide mineral, pyrite ("fool's gold"), is found in cubes (1) and also in an uncommon form known as the pyritohedron (2), so named because pyrite is the mineral in which

1. Pyrite · isometric · iron sulfide
Ambassaguas, Logrono, Spain

A cluster of several intergrown cubes of a mineral well known to collectors. Because of its brassy color and metallic luster, pyrite is often mistaken for gold, but simple tests showing its brittleness and high hardness reveal the difference. The cube is one of many crystal forms exhibited by pyrite. Although many other minerals have cubic crystals, pyrite can be easily identified by the presence of striations in different directions on adjacent faces.

2. Pyrite · isometric · iron sulfide

Butte, Silver Bow County, Montana

The intergrown crystals of this specimen are of the form known as the pyritohedron. The individual faces of this form are unusual in that they are five-sided polygons. Striations are present on these faces for the same reason that they appear on cube faces. The two forms, cube and pyritohedron, are in competition during growth, and the striations represent an alternate development of one form and then the other. The over-all shape of the crystal is determined by the form which is favored by growth conditions and therefore becomes dominant. In this example the pyritohedron is the dominant form. The minor tendency toward cube growth is revealed by the striations, which are actually very small segments of cube faces.

15

it is most frequently observed. Diamond (3) and franklinite (4) display another form often seen in isometric crystals, the octahedron. This eight-sided polyhedron resembles two square pyramids placed base to base. Leucite (5) shows yet another form of the isometric system, the trapezo-hedron, in which each face is shaped like a trapezium (a four-sided polygon with no two sides parallel). When two or more isometric forms are combined in a single crystal, the result looks rather complicated, as is well illustrated by the specimen of galena (6).

3. Diamond · isometric · carbon

Kimberley, Union of South Africa

This deformed octahedral crystal of diamond was exposed when a portion of the tightly enclosing matrix, a rock known as kimberlite, was broken away. Diamonds form under intense pressure at great depths within the earth. The edges of this crystal are beveled by minor development of another form, the trisoctahedron, so named because it looks like a modified octahedron in which each octahedral face is replaced by a very shallow pyramid made up of three triangular faces.

4. Franklinite · isometric · zinc iron oxide

Franklin, Sussex County, New Jersey

This crystal also shows a dominant octahedron, but the narrow planes along the edges indicate modification by a twelve-sided form called a dodecahedron. The names of minerals are usually derived from people, places, unusual properties, or from their composition. Franklinite was named for the locality where it was first discovered, in a zinc-iron-manganese mine.

17

If we imagine one axis of a cube shortened or elongated while the other two remain equal, the arrangement that results is characteristic of the tetragonal system (from *tetra* + *gonia* = four angles), illustrated by wulfenite (7). A set of three axes still at right angles to one another but all of different lengths characterizes the orthorhombic system (*ortho* + *rhombos* = straight rhomb). An ordinary brick possesses this symmetry, as does the mineral barite (8).

Crystal systems with mutually perpendicular axes are termed orthogonal; the isometric, tetragonal, and orthorhombic systems are all orthogonal. When one axis is inclined with respect to the other two, the resulting arrangement is characteristic of the monoclinic system (from *mono* = one + *clino* = inclined; one axis inclined), typified by the mineral gypsum (9). When all

5. Leucite · isometric · potassium aluminum silicate
Vesuvius, Italy

Natural crystals are often badly deformed, but this specimen of leucite, partially enclosed in the volcanic rock in which it grew, is a fine example of near-perfect development. Leucite is found only in extrusive volcanic rocks, since the conditions that favor its formation include high temperature and low pressure. This example is a trapezohedron, with twenty-four trapezium-shaped faces.

6. Galena · isometric · lead sulfide

Neudorf, Harz Mountains, Germany

One of the obvious properties used in characterizing minerals is luster. Galena
is a superb example of metallic luster; that is, luster resembling that of a metal. It
is heavy, as are most lead minerals, and is the principal ore of lead. This
particular crystal consists of three forms—cube, octahedron, and dodecahedron
—all developed to about the same extent.

19

7. Wulfenite · tetragonal · lead molybdate (above)

Los Lamentos, Chihuahua, Mexico

These lovely caramel-colored crystals look like flattened cubes. They formed in open cavities near the earth's surface by precipitation from solutions which attacked and dissolved other lead- and molybdenum-bearing minerals. The snow-white matrix upon which the crystals are perched is calcite, which was deposited in much the same way as the calcite making up stalactites and stalagmites in limestone caverns.

8. Barite · orthorhombic · barium sulfate (top, right)

Elk Creek, Meade County, South Dakota

If one were to bevel the edges of a brick, a geometrical solid resembling this crystal would be produced. This specimen was broken out of a nodule of fragmented limestone. The pale yellow crystals covering the surface of the limestone fragments are calcite. The luster of the barite is vitreous (glassy) and is due in part to its transparency. Specimens from Elk Creek are highly prized by collectors as perhaps the most beautiful of all barite crystals.

9. Gypsum · monoclinic · calcium sulfate hydrate (bottom, right)

Ellsworth, Mahoning County, Ohio

This transparent single crystal clearly illustrates the lower symmetry of the monoclinic system. The faces on either end, sloping in opposite directions, are usually indicative of crystals belonging to this group. Complete individuals like this one commonly form in clay, much as ice crystallizes in wet mud during the winter. Hardness is an important property in identifying gypsum; the mineral can be readily scratched with a fingernail.

three axes are inclined to one another, the resulting symmetry is called triclinic (*tri* = three), as seen in the mineral axinite (10).

Still another crystal system is characterized by three axes in a plane crossing at angles of 120 degrees to one another and a fourth axis perpendicular to the plane of the first three. The three planar axes are all the same

10. Axinite · triclinic · calcium aluminum borosilicate
St. Christophe, near Bourg d'Oisans, Isère, France

Triclinic crystals have axes of different lengths and different intersection angles. Therefore the symmetry of such crystals is of a very low order. Each crystal face slants obliquely away from all the others. The name axinite comes from *axine*, the Greek word for ax; its appropriateness is evident from the shape of the crystal. Since not many minerals form crystals of this shape, axinite usually can be identified on this basis.

length, but the fourth axis is either longer or shorter. The symmetry thus obtained is hexagonal (*hexa* + *gonia* = six angles). Many minerals crystallize in the hexagonal system; one of the most striking is the lead mineral pyromorphite (11). Although quartz (12) appears to be hexagonal, the outer form is deceptive. The atoms making up the internal structure of quartz are

11. Pyromorphite · hexagonal · lead chlorophosphate
Wheatley mines, Phoenixville, Chester County, Pennsylvania

This specimen consists of numerous crystals in the form of hexagonal prisms scattered about in random fashion. Those with their prism axes at a right angle from the plane of the photograph clearly reveal the six-sidedness of the prism. Regular crystals consisting only of a prism with a flat top and flat base are easy to recognize as hexagonal, but when the crystals are highly modified and badly deformed, hexagonal symmetry may be very difficult to establish by inspection.

12. Quartz · rhombohedral · silicon dioxide
Saint Gotthard, Switzerland

The lack of true hexagonal symmetry in quartz is evident from the fact that only the alternate faces of the six-sided pyramid that makes up the end of the crystal are approximately equal in development. Nearly always, three of the faces will be larger and three smaller, and these alternate around the pyramid. Each set of three equivalent faces is one half of a rhombohedron, a form resembling a distorted cube. This crystal is known as smoky quartz, in allusion to its color. In identifying quartz, color is of no importance because minute amounts of impurities may cause it to be nearly any color imaginable. The hardness of quartz exceeds that of glass; the mineral will readily scratch a window pane.

arranged in accordance with threefold symmetry, not sixfold, and quartz therefore belongs to the rhombohedral system (*rhombos + edron =* rhomb surfaces). Rhombohedral axes are the same as those of the hexagonal system, but rhombohedral minerals are characterized by threefold (trigonal) symmetry along the vertical axis rather than the sixfold symmetry of hexagonal minerals.

Twins

Intergrowths of two or more crystals of the same mineral sometimes obey specific laws, though randomly oriented groupings are more common. Crystals coming together on a plane which is clearly related to their atomic structure are called twinned crystals, the plane joining them is a twin plane, and the twin laws that describe the symmetry relationship between twinned individuals usually relate to a twin plane or a twin axis. The distinction between twinned crystals and random aggregates is sometimes hard to make, but the common occurrence of intergrown crystals of a mineral at a regular angle usually points to twinning. Some minerals twin so characteristically that this feature alone is a useful means of identification. This is true of the minerals rutile (13) and cerussite (14). Multiple twinning (involving more

13. Rutile · tetragonal · titanium dioxide
near Boiling Springs, Cleveland County, North Carolina

These crystals are so severely deformed and so deeply striated that their tetragonal character would be hard to determine by simple inspection. However, the color and the twinning are so characteristic that any experienced collector would immediately recognize the mineral. A network of many needlelike crystals joined at a constant angle is known as reticulated twinning.

than two individuals in a cyclic fashion) is seen in aragonite (15) and chrysoberyl (16). With these minerals the angle between the twinned crystals is close to 60 degrees, and the symmetry of the twin group is hexagonal, even though the individual crystals themselves are orthorhombic.

14. Cerussite · orthorhombic · lead carbonate
Tintic district, Utah

Another example of reticulated twinning. The individual crystals of which this group is composed can easily be seen to intersect at a regular angle, in this case 58°37′. Although it is a lead mineral, cerussite does not resemble a metal; in fact, its brilliant diamondlike luster is one of its most distinctive properties. However, the presence of lead is suggested by the great heaviness of the mineral.

15. Aragonite · orthorhombic · calcium carbonate

Agrigento, Sicily, Italy

Aragonite is the most common of several structurally similar carbonate minerals
known as the aragonite group. All have the tendency to form twins at an angle
of nearly 60°, and at times the twins consist of three crystals intergrown with a
common center so that the group resembles a six-rayed star. In the case of
aragonite, the lateral crystal faces commonly develop equally, and in joining
with their neighbors, they appear as one continuous face of each of the six sides
of a simple hexagonal crystal. Close inspection, however, will reveal sutures
where the individuals join and irregularities along the sides where adjacent faces
do not meet in perfect alignment.

27

16. Chrysoberyl · orthorhombic · beryllium aluminum oxide

near Collintina, Rio Doce, Espirito Santo, Brazil

This mineral twins in much the same way as aragonite. The six-rayed star formed by the intergrowth of three crystals at angles of almost 60° is obvious in this specimen, which is one of the finest known examples of multiple or cyclic twinning.

Deformed Crystals

Crystals "grown" in the laboratory are no longer a scientific curiosity. The term growth, as applied to crystals, refers to the slow, uniform deposition of chemical material on a nucleus, or "seed crystal." Such deposition usually occurs in water solutions, although it can proceed in melts, as is indeed the case in certain types of rocks which form at high temperatures. Under laboratory conditions, if the temperature, the purity of starting materials, and the conditions of growth are carefully controlled, very pure and perfectly formed crystals can be obtained. Conditions in nature are much more variable, so that natural crystals seldom exhibit idealized shapes. Many are so badly deformed that their true symmetry may be difficult to recognize. Crystals of the precious metals gold (17) and silver (18) are usually flattened and elongated, resembling sheets or branching and twisted wires. Copper,

17. Gold · isometric · gold
Grass Valley, Nevada County, California

Gold is a soft mineral but it is very resistant to the attacks of the agents of chemical weathering. Much of the gold that is mined is found in sands and gravels as fine flakes and rounded nuggets, in deposits known as placers. But if such gold could be seen in the rock in which it originally crystallized it might look very much like this specimen, a fine branching mass of platy crystals. This group probably formed in a narrow fracture in dense rock and therefore could grow only in the plane of the fracture. The crystal faces are sharp because the specimen was recovered in a gold mine in the solid rock of its origin (lode gold). Had it been freed by running water instead of by a miner's pick, it would have been bumped and pounded into a rounded nugget in a stream bed.

18. Silver · isometric · silver

Kongsberg, Norway

Silver, like gold, is isometric, but its crystals rarely exhibit much of the high symmetry of this crystal system. It is hard to imagine what conditions could have influenced the development of this fibrous-looking mass, but they must have been pervasive at Kongsberg because much of the silver from that mine is similarly distorted; examples from many other mines are also known. The mineral silver, like silverware in the home, tarnishes upon exposure to air, and its metallic luster soon becomes covered by a thin black coating.

a metal appreciated by collectors for the blue and green coloration it imparts to copper minerals, also tends to form distorted crystals (19).

Gypsum sometimes displays "kinked" crystals (20). The cause of these unusual modifications is not well understood but may be related to fluctuations in environmental conditions during or following growth.

By far the most common type of deformation in minerals is an inequality in the size of faces that on a perfect crystal would have developed equally.

19. Copper · isometric · copper
Keeweenaw Peninsula, Michigan

Copper is another isometric metal which, like silver and gold, is found in nature uncombined with other elements. These are known to mineralogists as native elements. These three minerals also have in common a tendency to appear in highly deformed crystals, softness, and the property of flattening out when hammered rather than breaking into tiny pieces as do brittle materials.

20. Gypsum · monoclinic · calcium sulfate hydrate

Friedrichroda, Thuringia, Germany

Looking somewhat like an inchworm about to move forward, this strange gypsum crystal has been kinked and bent through a process not completely understood. It has been suggested that the sharp changes in direction are due to glide twinning, a phenomenon resulting from the application of stresses to the crystal, such as might be caused by a closing of the walls of the cavity in which the crystal grew. This might have occurred through slow collapse of the cavity from the weight of material overhead.

Nearly every natural crystal suffers from deformation of this type. But a difference in the size of faces which under ideal conditions would be of equal size is an accident of growth and does not mean that the faces are not equivalent. One must overlook such imperfect growth in attempting to recognize the symmetry of a crystal. In this respect it is important to remember that the angles between equivalent faces on crystals of a given mineral are always the same, no matter how badly deformed the crystals may be. This fact enables one to identify minerals by measuring interfacial angles, even when the crystals are far from perfect.

Aggregates

Basically, minerals grow in the same way that a pile of dirt grows: new material is added to the surface and the mineral gradually becomes larger and larger. Conditions that are favorable for mineral growth are often conducive to the formation of many small crystals. These invariably grow into one another, producing random, subparallel, or parallel clusters.

If not too many crystal nuclei were formed initially, intergrowths with almost isolated crystals result. The aggregates of apophyllite (21), sulfur (22),

21. Apophyllite · tetragonal · hydrous potassium calcium fluorosilicate
Poona, India

A "triplet" of limpid green apophyllite crystals, with several isolated ones nearby, rests on a carpet of white zeolites. Although it does not belong to the zeolite group of minerals, apophyllite is very commonly found in association with these. It is one of several minerals for which the rocks of Deccan Plateau in India are famous. In that area there are thousands of square miles of basalt (traprock), liberally pockmarked with cavities, the walls of which are encrusted with marvelous crystals of apophyllite and of zeolite minerals, particularly stilbite and heulandite.

and wolframite (23) suggest that competition for space was not so keen that intergrowth completely inhibited good crystal development.

Prismatic minerals (so named because they are elongated in a direction parallel to one of the crystal axes) frequently grow in parallel to subparallel crystal bundles, as seen in tourmaline (24). Another type of prismatic aggregate is the result of radial growth from a common nucleus. Radial crystal

22. Sulfur · orthorhombic · sulfur
Agrigento, Sicily, Italy

Sulfur, oddly enough, may be any of three minerals; that is, depending upon the prevailing temperature, it may crystallize in three different atomic arrangements, designated as α-sulfur, β-sulfur, or γ-sulfur. The most common structure type is orthorhombic; this is usually referred to simply as sulfur. Crystals like those shown grow by condensation of sulfur vapors released by fumaroles in volcanically active areas. Sulfur is so heat-sensitive that if one holds a specimen very long the heat from the hand may be enough to crack it.

23. Wolframite · monoclinic · iron manganese tungstate

Panasqueira, Portugal

Some of the mineral specimens illustrated in this book are "old-timers," taken
long ago from mines that in most cases no longer exist. This one, however,
was mined within the past two years, and the mine from which it came is still
producing many fine specimens of wolframite, as well as other minerals. These
sharp and shiny tabular crystals grew randomly, with quartz, on the walls of
open fractures in rock, precipitated by metal-rich solutions moving
along the fractures.

24. Tourmaline · hexagonal · complex aluminum borosilicate

Santa Rosa mine, Minas Gerais, Brazil

Tourmaline is one of the loveliest of minerals, both for its fantastic variety of crystal formation and the way in which the colors change from end to end or from center to surface. It is common for tourmaline crystals to be bicolored—part one color and the rest another—and the variations often extend through more than two colors, including pinks, greens, and blues, and into numerous shades of each.

groups may contain well-formed isolated individuals, as in millerite (25), or the crystals may pack more closely together, as in pseudomesolite (26). Very dense accumulations, in which individuals are difficult to distinguish, are characteristic of the mineral pectolite (27). Fan-shaped arrangements of platy (layered) crystals, rather than needle-like ones, are well illustrated by the minerals autunite (28) and stilbite (29).

Masses of radial, compact groups of crystals that somewhat resemble bunches of grapes are termed botryoidal (from Greek *botrys*—grape). Smithsonite (30) and hematite (31) are two minerals that commonly occur in botryoidal groupings of crystals.

Irregularly intersecting crystal groups in which no arrangement of crystals can be detected are termed random intergrowths. Distinctive examples are found in stibnite (32), cerussite (33), and crocoite (34).

25. Millerite · rhombohedral · nickel sulfide
Sterling mine, Antwerp, Jefferson County, New York

The iron ore of the Sterling mine is bright red, earthy hematite, an oxide of iron. Numerous small cavities are scattered throughout the hematite and it is in these that delicate, needlelike crystals of millerite are found. The walls of the cavities are typically lined with black hematite in shiny flat plates, and buff-colored ankerite often later crystallizes on the hematite. The millerite needles tend to emanate radially from a single spot. Because of the delicacy of the crystals and the brassy, pyritelike color, millerite has been called "capillary pyrite."

26. Pseudomesolite · monoclinic · hydrous sodium calcium aluminum silicate

Ritter Hot Springs, Grant County, Oregon

Pseudomesolite is so named because it closely resembles another mineral called mesolite, differing only in optical properties. Mesolite derives its name from the fact that its composition is midway between those of two other similar zeolite minerals, scolecite and natrolite. Like all of these, pseudomesolite forms slender transparent or white crystals, which usually aggregate in radial balls, although individual crystals are discernible. Mesolite and pseudomesolite are known to occur together, and careful examination is required to distinguish between them.

27. Pectolite · monoclinic · hydrous sodium calcium silicate

Paterson, Passaic County, New Jersey

Mineral collectors who frequent the traprock quarries of northern New Jersey in search of zeolite minerals know, through painful experience, of the perfection of pectolite crystals which are found in abundance in this area. The balls of needles look as soft as tennis balls, but picking up a pectolite specimen carelessly is sure to result in numerous painful wounds from the tiny, sharply terminated crystals. Individual pectolite crystals are too small to be visible, but their presence can easily be felt, and most collectors are impaled by them before they learn how to handle this mineral.

28. Autunite · tetragonal · hydrous uranium calcium phosphate (above)

Daybreak properties, Mount Spokane area, Stevens County, Washington

Autunite is known as a secondary mineral, which means that it formed through alteration of another mineral, termed a primary mineral. The primary mineral which altered to provide the uranium to form autunite was uraninite, an oxide of uranium. Although uraninite is black, most secondary uranium minerals are brightly colored in shades of yellow and green. Autunite forms in a wet environment and water is an important part of its composition. When it is removed from the mine and placed in a home or museum where humidity is lower, it is unstable and loses at least half of its water. It adjusts to this water loss by changing its structure irreversibly to that of another mineral meta-autunite. Unfortunately for collectors, this change sets up strains within the crystals which usually result in their falling apart. To preserve autunite, it must be kept immersed in a liquid or given a coating that will prevent water loss.

29. Stilbite · monoclinic · hydrous sodium calcium aluminum silicate (right)

Prospect Park, Passaic County, New Jersey

One of the names given to stilbite centuries ago was "desmine" from the Greek *desmē*, meaning "bundle." In order to reduce confusion in mineral nomenclature, unnecessary synonyms are being discarded and the use of that name is now discouraged, but the photograph plainly shows why it was chosen. The group of tabular crystals appears to have been pulled in at the center and tied much like a bundle of wheat. This bizarre-seeming form is actually the way stilbite most often occurs.

30. Smithsonite · rhombohedral · zinc carbonate

Tsumeb, South-West Africa

Smithsonite is rarely found in simple isolated crystals, but it occurs in a great variety of other forms. Earthy-looking varieties are known, as well as crystalline crusts and stalactitic forms. Dull-surfaced incrustations of this type were known to early miners as "dry-bone ores," and indeed smithsonite has been mined for zinc, although it is not a major zinc-ore mineral. Another descriptive name is "turkey-fat ore" for yellow smithsonite. The more common form, however, is in rounded, nodular masses as pictured here. Minute impurities may color it many different hues, and, of these, deep blue and green are especially prized by collectors. Smithsonite was named in honor of James Smithson, the man whose gift made possible the founding of the Smithsonian Institution.

31. Hematite · rhombohedral · iron oxide

Cleator Moor, Cumberland, England

Though many hematite crystals are black, the powdered mineral reveals its true color, blood red, from which the name derives. In powdered form it has been used since early times as a paint pigment. A typical form for hematite is in smooth, rounded masses having almost an organic appearance; miners call it "kidney ore." Hematite is the most important source mineral for iron and provides more than 90 percent of the iron produced in North America.

32. Stibnite · orthorhombic · antimony oxide (top, left)

Iyo province, Shikoku Island, Japan

This mineral was named from its composition, but the connection is not obvious unless one knows that antimony was once called stibium. Although stibnite is a widespread and relatively common mineral, only a few localities have produced outstanding specimens. Of these, the Iyo province stibnites have consistently enjoyed the greatest fame. The mines there ceased production many years ago, and specimens can now be obtained only from the breaking up of old collections.

33. Cerussite · orthorhombic · lead carbonate (bottom, left)

Flux mine, Santa Cruz County, Arizona

"Jackstraws" is an appropriate metaphor for this random array of cerussite crystals. They exhibit all the disorder of a handful of straws thrown upon a flat surface. But, although the term is well suited to describe their arrangement, it does not explain how it came about. Like many secondary minerals, the cerussite grew out in all directions from the walls of a solution channel just below the earth's surface. Because the crystals are so long and slender they became complexly interwoven instead of forming a continuous lining along the walls. Of all the minerals found in such haphazard crystal groupings, the most dramatic and delicate are the cerussites from Arizona.

34. Crocoite · monoclinic · lead chromate (below)

Dundas District, Tasmania, Australia

This maze of crystals may also be described as a "jackstraw" grouping. Crocoite is among the minerals most sought by collectors. Its orange-red color is especially effective in displays, and it is also very rare. Since the few localities which produced specimens long ago ceased to do so, crocoite, like stibnite is available only when released from old collections.

Inclusions and Patterns

Although the conditions in which natural crystals grow may remain undisturbed for long periods of time, they sometimes change rapidly. The simultaneous deposition of two or more minerals sometimes occurs, as well as the deposition of one mineral quickly followed by that of another. Such intergrowths may form striking and beautiful patterns, with endless combinations.

Malachite and azurite (35), both carbonates of copper, commonly form nodular or concretionary masses. When sliced open, such masses reveal graceful swirls of blue and green banding that twist their way around concentric "bull's eyes" of the same minerals.

Cave visitors are familiar with the calcite formations called stalactites and stalagmites. Here carbonate minerals have been deposited in a concentric manner from evaporating solutions, and the tree-ring-like growths are easily seen in cross sections. When two carbonate minerals of different colors, such as white siderite and pink rhodochrosite (36), occur in alternating layers, the normally dull stalactite becomes a spectacular and beautiful natural object. Stalactites of goethite, an oxide of iron, are sometimes found lining the roof of a hollow concretion (37), the array of conical growths looking very much like an artist's conception of an extraterrestrial landscape.

35. Azurite and malachite · both monoclinic · both basic copper carbonates (top, right)
Bisbee, Cochise County, Arizona

These two copper minerals, so different in color, are almost identical in composition and are almost always found together in secondary copper mineral assemblages. Azurite, as its name implies, is blue, and malachite is green. Minor changes in conditions during crystallization can cause the formation of one mineral to be favored over the other. This specimen is a polished section through a knobby crust made up of concentric layers of azurite and malachite. Each of the "bull's-eyes" represents a symmetrical hemispherical or tubular growth. The irregular patterns are produced when two or more of these come together in growing.

36. Rhodochrosite and siderite · both rhombohedral · manganese carbonate and iron carbonate, respectively (bottom, right)
Catamarca province, Argentina

Rhodochrosite and siderite are similar chemically, in that they are both carbonate minerals, and structurally they are identical. Rhodochrosite, a manganese carbonate, is pink to red. Siderite, an iron carbonate, may range in color from nearly white to dark brown. This specimen is a polished section of two coalescing stalactitic groups. The sharp definition of the concentric layering comes about because some layers are white siderite, some pink rhodochrosite, and others a pale pink intermediate carbonate containing both manganese and iron. Such growths of these minerals are extremely rare and this occurrence in Argentina may even be unique; it is made even more unusual by the fact that a layer of pyrite was deposited near the very last stages of growth.

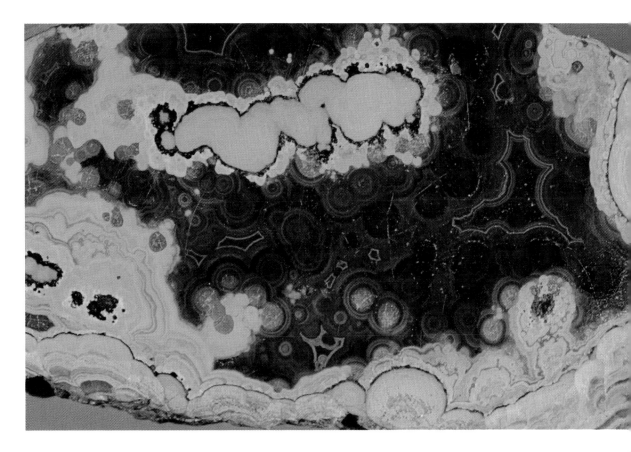

Rutilated quartz (38) forms in two stages. Masses of delicate needlelike rutile crystals grow first and at some later time are enclosed by crystals of water-clear quartz. Quartz, a tough, resistant mineral, preserves the fragile shafts of rutile which could never survive as free-standing crystals.

Cracks sometimes develop during the formation of a mineral, proving easy access for solutions that deposit other minerals or react with existing minerals to form new ones later. The process of cracking and filling may be repeated several times, resulting in a lacy network of color such as is seen in variscite nodules (39).

37. Goethite · orthorhombic · iron hydroxide
Herdorf, Westphalia, Germany

This specimen resembles the roof of a limestone cavern with numerous calcite stalactites suspended from it. However, these growths are less than an inch in length and they are not calcite, but goethite. If one of these "pencil points" were broken off, the break would reveal a spokelike radial pattern of tightly compacted goethite crystals quite unlike the concentric layering one sees in stalactites (see 36). This massive black goethite looks very much like hemitite (see 31), but the two minerals can readily be distinguished by powdering small pieces; goethite powder is yellowish-brown, hematite red.

38. Rutile (in quartz) · tetragonal · titanium oxide
Itibiara, Bahia, Brazil

Crystals frozen in quartz are literally what this specimen shows. Extremely delicate rutile needles grew into an open cavity, perhaps filled with liquid or with silica gel. These crystals are so long and slender that, unprotected, they would shatter at the least tremor, and consequently they could never be mined intact from the enclosing rock. Fortunately, however, they became encased in transparent quartz and were thus preserved to be admired by man. This locality has produced countless tons of quartz crystals containing rutile crystals, some specimens weighing at least 100 pounds. Often the crystal faces of such quartz are too imperfect to serve as good windows for revealing their wondrous interiors and must be ground flat and polished.

49

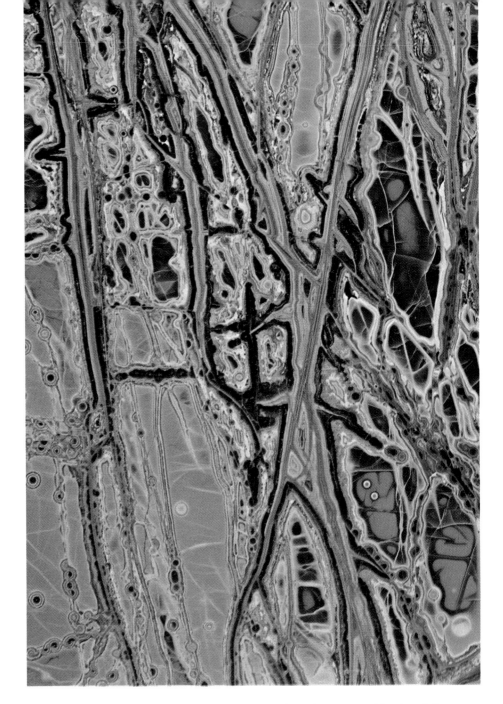

39. Variscite and crandallite · aluminum phosphate hydrate and basic calcium aluminum phosphate hydrate, respectively

near Fairfield, Utah County, Utah

Surprisingly, this beautiful specimen is a section cut through the interior of a dull-gray, earthy nodule. Large numbers of nodules of green variscite formed in this locality from the circulation of phosphatic ground water through a brecciated (broken-up) limestone. Subsequent fracturing of the nodules permitted later solutions to penetrate and react with the variscite. Since the new solutions were not phosphorus-bearing but were calcium-rich, the reaction produced a new mineral, buff-colored crandallite, along the fractures and at the surface of the nodule. Many other minerals were also formed, but in small amounts compared to the great abundance of variscite and crandallite.

Pseudomorphs and Replacements

In nature, change is always taking place, though the rate may be extremely slow. The stability of a mineral in its environment is often short-lived; as conditions change, the mineral may begin to dissolve and be replaced by another that is more stable in the new conditions. The replacement may occur so slowly that the outlines of the first-formed mineral are preserved in the process. The newly deposited material thus exhibits the outer form of a different substance, long since dissolved away. An example of such a pseudomorph is stibiconite after stibnite (40). In the specimen in which the deep blue crystals of azurite are only partially replaced by green malachite (41) the replacement process was interrupted, thus providing evidence that

40. Stibiconite · antimony oxide
Catorce, San Luis Potosi, Mexico

The crystal form seen here is that of stibnite, a sulfide of antimony. Since stibnite is lead-gray with a bright metallic luster (see 32), the original mineral has obviously been altered. It has, in fact, been completely replaced by another mineral, stibiconite, an oxide of antimony. This is an example of the type of pseudomorph that involves a partial exchange of constituents. The antimony ions may be considered to have remained, while sulfur was removed and oxygen took its place.

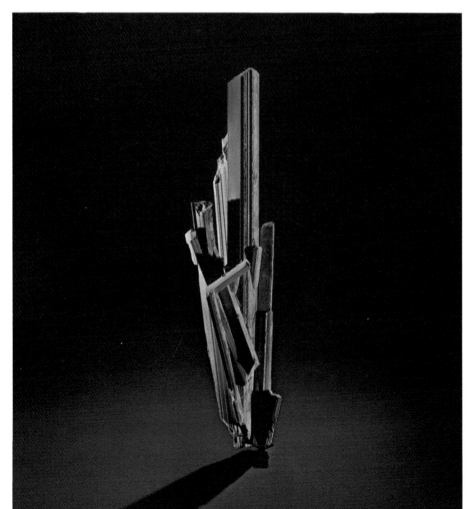

41. Malachite replacing azurite · both monoclinic · both basic copper carbonates
Tsumeb, South-West Africa

Malachite, commonly found with azurite (see 35), is in this instance actually replacing the latter. The beautiful 7-inch azurite crystal was removed in mining before the alteration had proceeded very far. The green film of malachite is not a coating but a partial replacement. Many complete pseudomorphs of malachite after azurite have been recovered at Tsumeb. Though mining still continues there, these specimens were found only in an upper zone long since mined out; no azurite or malachite has been encountered for many years.

it was going on. However, when no crystal forms are present to indicate the prior existence of a mineral replaced by another, the process may be difficult to establish with certainty.

A different and very obvious type of replacement occurs with petrified wood, in which the original woody material has been carried away in solution and its place taken by a mineral. A microscopic section of petrified wood may reveal perfectly the original organic cell structure, now preserved in mineralogical permanence, as in the specimen of oak replaced by quartz (42).

42. Quartz (petrified oak wood) · silicon dioxide

Clover Creek, Lincoln County, Idaho

Wood is sometimes buried in sand and clay where it is subjected for millions of years to the action of slowly moving solutions. The solutions contain dissolved mineral materials, especially silica (silicon dioxide), and the wood acts as a sponge so that all openings between cell walls are gradually filled by mineral. Later the cell walls themselves may be dissolved away and these areas filled also. What remains is a replica in stone of even the minutest structures of the original woody material. The presence of impurities, such as oxides of iron, may add bright color to the petrified wood and intensify the detail of the woody structure.

Pseudo-organic Aggregates

To most people, certain types of patterns suggest familiar organic forms; for example, a branching, lacy design is associated with tree branches and the veins of leaves. Some mineral formations, however, so strikingly resemble characteristic organic patterns that for hundreds of years they were regarded as fossils. The dendritic pattern is duplicated by creeping films of manganese-oxide-bearing solutions that dry up within very thin rock fissures (43). Diffusion of colored mineral-bearing solutions into silica gel results in plantlike and feathery-looking growths, causing the solidified rock to be called moss agate, feather agate, or plume agate. Gold, silver, and copper can occur in treelike formations (see 17, 18, 19), but the treelike patterns in some agates are much more realistic (44).

43. Psilomelane · orthorhombic · basic barium, manganese oxide
Lavalleja Department, Uruguay

A common feature of many stratified sedimentary rocks such as sandstone, shale, and limestone is their tendency to break apart into platy slabs with perfectly planed surfaces. Before these rocks are exposed so that they may be separated, tiny fractures exist in the otherwise massive rock, revealing its readiness to produce flat slabs. Solutions carrying dissolved minerals can penetrate these cracks and spread out within them. With saturation, crystals of the dissolved minerals, psilomelane in this case, grow in branching forms in the plane of the fractures because the solutions cannot penetrate the dense, nonporous rock. When the rock is split along the cracks one never knows how exciting a pattern will be revealed.

44. Quartz (dendritic agate) · silicon dioxide
India

Agate, a very abundant form of the mineral quartz, is composed of tiny fibrous crystals, individually invisible except under very high magnification. Such masses are termed cryptocrystalline, and the manner in which the crystals interlock makes agate extremely tough. Most agate contains impurities that were incorporated in various stages of its formation. Sometimes solutions containing iron or manganese creep into thin fractures in almost hardened agate; the solutions then evaporate to leave films of black or red oxides of these metals. The irregular films sometimes resemble natural objects or scenes, such as trees and mountainous landscapes. The "dendritic" agates of India are among the finest known.

Crystal aggregates may also resemble flowers, as seen in the mineral barite (45). The resemblance is so striking and examples similar to this one are so abundant at certain localities that these groups have become widely known to collectors as "desert roses." Under other conditions barite may take on the appearance of a full, bushy evergreen shrub (46). The radial spray of marcasite crystals (47) may be compared to a common flower, though the resemblance is entirely fortuitous.

Such unusual mineral formations remind the viewer of the unity of natural forces. The same laws that have caused evolution to produce life in its known forms are at work in the realm of inorganic matter as well. The similarities in form that result are striking evidence of the underlying order of the universe.

The mineral kingdom is as varied as it is vast. In some ways it is like human society, in that it presents a panorama of the rare and the common, the beautiful and the grotesque, the simple and the complex. As with people, the development of minerals is greatly influenced by the environment in which they grow. Some minerals are so characteristic of certain types of rocks that they always carry unmistakable indications of their birthplace. Other minerals are so common and their appearance so undistinctive that one could not hope to pinpoint their place of origin. Yet all minerals have certain characteristics by which they can be readily identified.

45. Barite · orthorhombic · barium sulfate

near Norman, Cleveland County, Oklahoma

Barite usually forms tabular (table-shaped) crystals, and these sometimes grow in clusters from a common center, resulting in an aggregate that looks like a rose. The normal high luster of barite is lacking in this specimen because, instead of developing in an open cavity, it grew through porous sand, gradually filling the openings and in so doing cementing the surrounded sand grains together. Since the surface of the crystals is partly barite and partly sand grains, the "petals" have the appearance of sandpaper.

46. Barite · orthorhombic · barium sulfate

near Cave in Rock, Hardin County, Illinois

This specimen shows another type of barite clustering, reminiscent of a dense evergreen shrub. The bushiness is due to branching of subparallel groups of platy crystals, but only scattered flashes of light from small faces indicate the real nature of the mass.

   Some properties such as color and shape, may vary, but others are always the same. Every mineral has a color, which in itself may or may not be indicative of the species. Every mineral breaks in a characteristic way, either with flat, regular partings or with uneven surfaces. Most significantly, every mineral has an internal structure which causes it to form in the specific crystal type that mineralogists have learned to associate with it. The structures are very characteristic of the individual minerals, and so, therefore, are the crystals. In fact, the science of crystal measurement is so well developed that many substances can be identified on the basis of a few measurements of the angles between crystal faces.

When you see a person you know, your brain associates a name with the collection of features which serve to distinguish this individual. Minerals can become familiar in much the same way—through constant association. The more often you see a particular type of mineral, the simpler it is to identify it. Some minerals are easier to recognize than others, as might be guessed from the unusual forms pictured in this book. But pictures are no substitute for reality, and no picture can quite do justice to the physical object itself. Minerals are displayed in many museums and are there to be looked at. After sufficient acquaintance, the prominent members of the remarkable mineral society will indeed become old and familiar acquaintances.

47. Marcasite · orthorhombic · iron sulfide
Lyme Regis, Dorset, England

It seems almost incredible that any process except fossilization could produce the extraordinary likeness to a living flower displayed by the arrangement of these crystals. This specimen is not unique; Lyme Regis has produced a number of these "flowers."

Bibliography

Dana, Edward R., and Hurlbut, C. S. Jr. *Manual of Mineralogy.* 17th rev. ed. New York: Wiley, 1959.
  A popular, nontechnical introduction to mineralogy used extensively both as a college textbook and as a permanent reference by collectors. Approximately 200 minerals are extensively described and many more mentioned briefly.

Desautels, P. E. *The Mineral Kingdom.* Photographs by Lee Boltin. New York: Grosset and Dunlap, 1968.
  A presentation of romantic legends and contemporary stories revealing the fascination of the world of minerals. Illustrated with more than 140 color and a large number of black and white photographs.

Ford, W. E. *A Textbook of Mineralogy.* New York: Wiley, 1932.
  Extensive treatment of mineralogy and crystallography with descriptions of all the minerals known at the time of publication. In spite of being dated, this book continues to be one of the most important references for the serious collector.

Hurlbut, C. S., Jr. *Minerals and Man.* New York: Random House, 1968.
  Describes the nature and origin of many of the world's important mineral deposits together with stories of how the minerals have been and are being used. Illustrated with more than 150 color and many more black and white photographs.

Mason, B., and Berry, L. G. *Elements of Mineralogy.* San Francisco: W. H. Freeman, 1968.
  Easily read, nontechnical but comprehensive introductory textbook in the study of minerals. Some 200 minerals are described in detail.

Pearl, R. M. *How to Know the Minerals and Rocks.* New York, McGraw-Hill, 1955.
  An illustrated field guide to more than 125 familiar minerals and rocks.

————. *Rocks and Minerals.* New York: Barnes and Noble, 1956. (Everyday Handbooks—paperback.)
  A comprehensive, lucidly written survey of mineralogy, crystallography, geology, gemology, economic geology, and meteorites, for readers of all ages.

Pough, F. H. *Field Guide to Rocks and Minerals.* Boston: Houghton Mifflin, 1955.
  Simplified field guide designed to aid the amateur in the identification of the most common minerals and rocks.

Sinkankas, J. *Mineralogy: A First Course.* Princeton, N.J.: Van Nostrand, 1966.
  Informal introductory textbook, perhaps easier than most texts for the amateur to comprehend.

Zim, H. S., and Shaffer, R. R. *Rocks and Minerals.* New York: Golden Books, 1957. (Paperback.)
  Elementary guide, excellent for young collectors and for adults with a casual interest in rocks and minerals.

Index

62

About the Photographer

Lee Boltin is a freelance photographer whose photographs and films of natural-history subjects have won awards given by the National Urban League, the Edinburgh Film Festival, and the Graphic Arts Award Competition. His photographs have appeared in *Smithsonian, Horizon, Natural History,* and *Scientific American,* as well as in a number of books.

About the Author

John S. White, Jr., received his B.S. in Geology from Franklin and Marshall College, Lancaster, Pennsylvania, in 1956, and his M.S. in Mineralogy from the University of Arizona in 1966. He joined the Smithsonian Institution in the Division of Mineralogy in 1963.

A member of the Mineralogical Society of America, he is also the editor-publisher of *Mineralogical Record,* and has contributed articles to *American Mineralogist* and *Science* magazines.